Oh, So Delicious!
And Healthy, Too!™

SUSAN ANDERSON- COONS

ILLUSTRATED BY SHARON BACKUES

www.trafford.com

North America & international
toll-free: 1 888 232 4444 (USA & Canada)
phone: 250 383 6864 ♦ fax: 812 355 4082

Oh, So Delicious! And Healthy, Too! ™

By: Susan Anderson-Coons

Illustrations by Sharon Backues

First Edition.

Oh, So Delicious! And Healthy, Too Cookbook.
Raw Foods + Handy Tips.

An Out of the Box Look at Ways to Use Raw and Other Healthy Foods

Preface: Why Do We Do This?

How any times do we wonder about the rising cost of medical care?

We see friends and relatives on prayer lists that face medical bills that affect their financial survival. The media discusses this health crisis daily.

The good news is that recent research offers hope. Doctors in medical schools now take classes in "Glycobiology," the science of how cells burn sugars and how our body uses foods. It tracks how cells talk to each other and how the body heals itself. When we eat "junk" food, we develop unprotected, weak cells. This and stress are factors which drain nutrients from cells. Good food builds cell strength. Poor sources drain cell strength. You may ask, "What's new about that?"

In recent years, scientists have studied cells with a better microscope. They learned more about what we eat and what that knowledge can do for us. That research has given us more tools for a healthier lifestyle.

Even "eating well" and getting clean water is not as simple as once thought. When food is picked green, if it sits in stores that are sprayed, we might still face pollution. Cell research shows that some of 8 nutrients around each cell needed for cell defense are often missing. Scientists even have a clearer picture of how body cells talk to each other through "intercellular communication."

At a recent Mannatech conference in Medford, Oregon, Dr. John Axford, retired head of the U.S. Patent Office, called this discovery of Glycobiology , a "21st Century breakthrough." Dr. Axford labeled it, a "Disruptive Technology", comparable to disruptive technologies like the invention of radio, TV, printing press, and nuclear energy. Axford said that how cells communicate and what they need for cell health changes the way many professionals see health and wellness.

Scientists studying people around the world who live long, healthy lives find that for the healthy ones, eight essential sugars are on each cell.

Often, some of these "sugars" are not on the cells of people less long lived. These sugars surround cells with a sticky web-like substance that tells cells what to repair or flush. Called "intercellular communication," this process is like writing a letter with half of the alphabet. It results in the body repairing or flushing the wrong things. This may explain why just having "wealth" does not always guarantee us the quality of health of some "primitive societies" where the natives live long, healthy lives. The USA is one of the richest nations in the world, but it is 63rd from the top in health.

We sometimes hear, "Without a vision, the people perish." We can change that by taking action to reduce our part in this USA statistic. How?

1. Maintain a diet of organic, fresh foods.

2. Find sources for clean water. Drink 8 glasses of water/day.

3. Learn about low glycemic eating from the internet at sites such as <glycoscience.com> or a get a booklet at a health food store.

4. Cut back on fried, fatty foods.

5. Focus on organic legumes, raw fruits, vegetables, flaxseed, grains, celery, eggs, chocolate, green tea, kefir, yogurt, dairy, organic meats & poultry, soy, protein shake, nutritional supplements as suggested by World Health Organization. If you have food sensitivities, check with your physician.

6. Get regular exercise.

7. Stay informed with latest studies on nutrition as science develops. That research on your part keeps you on the cutting edge concerning your own health choices. The reward? A possibility for greater vitality and wellness in later years. Wouldn't that be great?

Tip: To keep kitchen and bathroom sponges and scrubbers fresh, place them in the dishwasher on a regular basis. That gives you one more way to keep those nasty germs out of your home without using harsh chemicals.

Chapter One: Healthy Breakfasts. Start the Day with Clean Water.

As officials grow aware of maintenance challenges facing water companies to keep water pure, more people are adding a water filtration system to their water supply. Some are concerned enough to purify outlets into their bathrooms also, even as they wait for science to solve this challenge. Newscasters tell about failing water systems in parts of North America that need to be strengthened. The power of the USA and Canada historically has been with creative, problem solving minds. We will solve this problem as we have other challenges in the past. While waiting, here are some options:

1. New Wave water purifier system. Sold at health food stores, this one lets the consumer have a system at a reduced cost, even if it does not have the number of third party studies completed that Multipure has at this time. One consideration for **New Wave** is that it does have a 10 stage filtration system, which may have the potential to filter more debris.

2. Multipure is one of the water purifiers that has had an independent Third Party Laboratory testing. This Testing Lab gave them high purification ratings for effectiveness in cleansing the water. One reason given is that Multipure uses a solid carbon block that has been tested for effectiveness. One facet of Multipure marketing is that it is sold through a Multi-Level Marketing system. A person using its many made in USA products can also attend meetings and get questions answered.

A critical point for any of these purifiers is that the filters need to be replaced on a scheduled basis, as suggested by each water filtration company.

3. Another purifier used by Dr. Milner's office in Portland, Oregon is **Ionways**. Dr. Milner is Medical Advisor for the Advisory Panel for Health Science Institute and President of the National College for Natural Medicine. He teaches Cardiology in addition to his practice in Portland, Oregon. Dr. Milner can be reached at 1-503-232-1100.

4. Easy Water is a purifier that has been available for over 25 years. For extensive details on this one, check <easy water.com>.

In addition to the above references, find out what is available in your area. *"If we keep doing what we have always done, we will get what we have always gotten."* In this era with water and other health problems mentioned in the news —we can't afford to linger longer.

This is not a definitive list of water purifier systems. Your water may have special needs. What you do to tailor your purifier to fit those needs might make a difference. *Should you purchase any of the above or some other system like the systems sold in markets, you need to follow the instructions in the guides that come with the units and do the research for one that fits your needs. Check local sources and ask questions.*

LeRoy's Granola Breakfast Boost

     1. Use 1 3/4 cup organic oats and 1/4 cup organic barley flakes for 2 cups of a cereal blend. White rice has a high glycemic index like white sugar and is best not used.

     2. Add 1/2 cup mixed nuts

     3. 1/4 cup raisins

     4. 1/4 cup banana chips

     5. 1/8 cup dried chopped papaya.

     6. To Prepare: Blend above ingredients in food processer or a food chopper until lightly chopped.

Recipe keeps well. Extra portion can be frozen for later use.
Store in a large jar at room temperature.

     For a breakfast cereal, 1/4 cup of mixture in bowl with 1/2 cup of goat milk, cow's milk or coconut milk. Soak in the milk for ten minutes at breakfast time for a tasty raw cereal or cook gently for 5 minutes. You can add honey, agave or Stevia for sweetener.

     Some who tried this didn't want added sweetener. Note: Oats make great muffins when used as a substitute for flour in a muffin recipe. They offer an energy boost that can carry you through the morning, while still having an organic start to the day.

Tip for the Day: "Live like each day is your last." --LeRoy F. Hawkins 2011

Kava, Green Tea, Black Tea, Coffee & Chocolate.

The drinks that we use with our meals will vary based on habits and culture. They can be helpful or harmful. For example, concerning drinks that contain artificial red coloring made up of phenols, it makes sense to know what you are drinking. Some of these phenols can be harmful over time. Phenols are poisonous, corrosive, crystalline acid compounds…used as disinfectant (Webster's Collegiate Dictionary). In the area of teas and coffees, an awareness of the effect of the drinks can be a factor in making your beverages work for you or against you. Below is a sample of drinks, but it would take another book to show all of the ways that you can use them to your advantage.

1. Kava is a calming tea used in the Polynesian Islands. It was part of native religious ceremonies and is drunk today in the USA by some for its soothing effects. "Pili Pili" was another name for it and it was given to Polynesian children as a vitamin.

2. Coffee was used in Europe, Scandinavian and North and South American countries for years. It is still sipped in small "cafés" where students gather to discuss political or social events. The varieties of coffee are based on where the coffee beans are grown. Coffee may be a problem for some people, but it may lend energy or be a mood lifter. If you have questions about this, check with your physician and with books such as **Bottom Line's Healing Remedies or Jean Carper's The Food Pharmacy, a book favorably reviewed by Prevention Magazine.**

3. Teas have been an important part of British culture, in the USA and Canada and are part of the meal for some. Recently, the effect of drinking green tea to help the body speed up weight loss has become popular. Black teas are a staple for others with an energy boost like that of coffee. Again, if you have questions about a tea, check with your doctor.

4. We enjoy hearing that chocolate is considered good for health. Hot chocolate is a favorite drink and the use of Truvia, Stevia (tiny amounts of Stevia) or American grown Xylitol can sweeten a hot chocolate while keeping down the daily sugar intake and calories. For more information, see books listed above or check **Pages 39, 45 and 65. They show ideas on how to change your favorite chocolate recipe into a wholesome version that cuts down on the use of sugars by substituting some of the more wholesome sweeteners listed on page 44.** This cookbook does not cover all options in this area. It is an effort to help you find ways to change favorite foods that might be harmful into healthy alternatives and encourage you to become your own sleuth and healthy food adapter.

Yogurt Shake. Breakfast Boost.

1. *1/2 cup skimmed milk or 1/2 cup yogurt per person. Greek yogurt works well. Some people use goats' milk, soy yogurt, and kefir or soy milk, if they have a dairy allergy.*

2. 1 scoop of *whey protein drink mix.*

3. One scoop of *chia seeds* from Health Food Store.

4. Add *1/2 cup frozen blueberries, frozen strawberries* or other fruit. The frozen fruit makes this taste more like a sherbet.

5. **A variety of powdered nutritional supplements** add protein energy to this drink. Some optional supplements come from companies such as Mannatech, IVL, Trivita, Kyani. Below are resources that can be used for breakfast.

A. 2 Tbsp. of Trivita's Nopalea—a nutritious *fruit from Nopal Cactus juice* found in the desert. Their B vitamins can be helpful. **See Resources. P.66.**

B. 2 Tbsp. of *Lily of the Desert Aloe Vera Gel.* You may use other companies, but this gives you an idea. Check Health Food Stores or use resources at the back of the book.

C. 1 tsp. *Mannatech's Ambrotose plus the addition of Glycolean.* (Whirled in the blender, this forms an energy drink with pure foods that for some cuts cravings for more fattening foods. **See Resources. P. 66.**

D. Kyani is a food source using ingredients gathered by the Tlingit tribe in Alaska. USDA reports that a high percent of the US population gains less than 70% of the nutrients needed to maintain health. With high ORAC ratings in the Kyani Company's products, many note a dramatic energy boost and a cut back on inflammation. D, C & B deficiencies are common. **See Resources on P. 66.**

Tip: When the Mannatech or Kyani mixture is frozen with a banana blended into the mixture, it makes a sherbet for you and family without having others suspect that it is "good "for them. Protein shakes with vitamin supplements also help some people to lose pounds. If allergic sensitivities, this can be modified using goat, rice or soy milk to keep allergen level lower. Whey protein powder also works for some and can be found in health food sections of many stores. **If you have questions, check with your Physician or one who understands nutrition. Also, check Resources on P. 66.**

Yogurt Shake (Continued)

When my children were pre-school age dealing with daily croup sessions, we took them to a San Francisco medical center. A doctor ran tests and found allergies. He offered an approach to their health that changed the way that I viewed illness and health. He showed me a glass of water and said that a sensitive person's body is like having a glass partially full or overflowing with allergy causing substances. Many people aren't bothered by such factors, because trigger factors are low enough to handle the irritants. For others, the irritants overflow their tolerance level like a full glass of water to cause reactions. For serious allergies, even one contact with an allergen creates life threatening reactions. As a result of that testing, I changed their diet to non-wheat; non-dairy and wiped down the walls for mold and dust. A change took place in their health. This began an interest in another. As we keep environmental issues for health and well-being. We all have a journey tailored to our needs. One principle is to tune into our body and soul and find what we need for health and spiritual being. **What works for one person may be different for another. As we keep up that sleuthing we may find what we need for wellness.** As for the yogurt shake, there are many versions that boost energy, but the frozen banana or a similar fruit like a frozen papaya, blueberries or strawberries, etc., help to make it creamy like ice cream sherbet.

Muffin Meal Morsel.

A. In Mixmaster place ground flours. Mix well before adding nuts, liquids and fruits.

Organic ingredients preferred:

1. One cup gluten free wheat// or: grind 1 cup oats in blender until flour like consistency.

2. Add one of these grains: 1 cup rye flour, 1 cup oat bran. Then add: 1/2 cup flax or chia seeds.

3. 1 tbsp. cinnamon

4. 1/2 cup agave or honey. See Page 44 "Sweeteners."

Also: If you prefer stevia or truvia or Xylitol, Add 2-4 Tbsp. sweetener to taste.

5. 1 tsp. baking powder and 1 tsp. baking soda

B. Add to ingredients above:

1. 1 cup ground almonds or walnuts

2. 1 cup cranberries, raisins or coconut flakes

3. 1 cup lactose free milk, or yogurt or goat milk

4. 4 large eggs

5.1 cup blueberries or other fruit

6. 1/3 cup coconut oil or 1/2 cup butter

7. 1 tbsp. vanilla.

C. Combine liquids and fruit mashed in a blender. Stir in dry ingredients. Spoon into 8 x 12 pan or muffin cups.

Bonus Tip: Increase milk, yogurt or goat milk to 1 1/2 cups milk for pancakes or waffles.

D. Bake at 350 degrees for 20 - 25 minutes until a knife comes out clean. This can be a bake-ahead meal when in a hurry or as a weekend breakfast treat. The muffins freeze well for a nutritious reserve for later breakfasts on the run.

Zucchini Surprise Bread

Pre-Heat oven to 400 degrees:

1. Ingredients:

2 cups oatmeal or bran flakes blended to flour consistency.

1/2 cup sesame seeds = optional for added flavor.

1 tsp. baking powder

1 tsp. cinnamon

1 tsp. nutmeg

1/2 tsp. salt

1/4 cup yogurt

 2 eggs

1/2 cup melted butter

1 cup agave or honey when agave is not available

1/4 cup Stevia or other sugar substitute may be use

2 cups zucchini grated in food processor

1 cup cranberries or raisins

1 cup diced almonds or pecans.

2. Steps.

Step 1. Whirl oatmeal or bran in blender to make fine flour.

Step 2. Grate zucchini.

Step 3. In Mixmaster, combine Steps 1&2.

Step 4. Add cinnamon, nutmeg, agave, butter yogurt, egg, sesame seeds, and baking powder. Once blended, add cranberries or raisins and nuts.

Step 5. Pour into 8 x 12 pan coated with olive oil or Pam. Can also use for cupcakes. Bake 35-40 minutes for 8 x 12 or 20-25minutes for cupcakes at 350 degrees.

Tip: When God wants our attention, He gives us a nudge. If we ignore Him, He often reminds us again. If we still ignore Him, He leaves us to our own devices, which may include disasters. We sometimes forget that He is jealous of His sovereignty and does not want us upstarts to ignore Him.

Oatmeal Waffles

1. Into blender grind two cups oats with 1/2 cup nuts until it is a flour like consistency.

2. Melt 1/2 cup melted butter on stove. Add 1/2 cup milk to cool mixture.

3. Add 3 large eggs whipped into butter and milk.

4. Add flour, butter and eggs in mixmaster.

5. Add 1 cup organic yogurt.

6. Add 1 tsp. baking powder, 1/2 tsp. salt

7. Check consistency. If too runny for waffles, add 1/2 cup more of unground oats to batter.

8. Pour 1/2 cup batter into waffle iron and cook.

9. Serve with honey or agave.

Tip: You can vary this by adding blueberries or other fruit instead of nuts to batter.

When Life Gives Us Lemons ...

Make Lemonade. A tidbit of food plus a bit of philosophy.

We can turn those lemons into lemonade and learn the joy of warm vinegar & honey to start the day. On a practical basis, in 2005, Bottom Line's book <u>Healing Remedies</u> listed 36 health uses for lemons alone as a source of wellness. One way to enjoy the benefits of lemons on a daily basis might be a warm cup of lemonade and honey. Try the following: ***<u>Juice of one lemon sweetened with 1 Tbsp. of honey to taste</u>*** Avoid zest of lemon due to sprays in some orchards. <u>Prevention Magazine</u> writes that lemons keep us more resistant to infections.

A psychological part of what we face is to think of how we react when we face "life lemons." At those times, it might help to reach out to others. For some, professional counseling might lend perspective. Sometimes, we can use challenges to grow.

1. For some, prayer support helps. "If two or more agree as touching any matter, I'll be there, hear and answer" is a promise from God in the <u>Old Testament</u>. Handling challenges with grace helps us to see how God uses the "foolish things of the world for good."

2. Another way to handle conflicts is to find ways to handle criticism. When we go to a critic, acknowledge the concern and work on the issue, we grow. This often builds a bridge. If not, we are not then responsible for the other person's reaction.

3. Sometimes, challenges occur where we pushed our agenda and forgot the other person's needs. Knowing this, we can change our part of the process and accept what we can't change as described in the classic "Serenity Prayer. By offering forgiveness and love when there might be reason to be angry is one way to turn sour lemons into lemonade. For those eager to grasp the deeper purposes of life, -- might that not be why we are here on earth? --- **One challenge on the wall of a cafe:** *To Live, To Listen, To Forgive, To Love and To Give.*

4. Odd Ideas that work-- from our household to yours. Once your household gets used to exploring new adventures, add lecithin and almond butter to your muffin recipe. If family members are stuck on old cake mix tastes, try a chocolate cake where you slip in 1/2 cup slivered almonds, 1/8 cup lecithin, 1/2 cup chia seeds, 1/2 cup cranberries into the mix. Use yogurt instead of the water or milk that are indicated in many cake recipes. If you substitute butter for the shortening of some recipes, you will get a rich taste without as many trans fats. It would be good to avoid the cake mix, but work with your household one step at a time. A fresh approach to food might take time for some to learn. In the long run, they might like it. It is worth a try.

Lemon Recipes

Lemonade can be a morning wake-up drink. Since lemon is acidic, brushing teeth can keep the teeth more free of acid corrosion. You can sip the lemon-honey drink for Vitamin C as a start to the day.

Lemony Ice Cream

2 squeezed lemons, 1 frozen banana. Keep bananas stored in freezer for ice cream variations.

1 cup organic yogurt or organic Greek yogurt. Place in freezer until frozen. 2 hours.

1/4 cup Xylitol, 2 tbsp. Ambrotose from Mannatech

2 tbsp. Glycogen Shake powder from Mannatech.

Place in blender and mix. Place in bowl in freezer until ready to use.

Flush grumpy germs into the sink with tasty lemon treats. "Say 'Yes' to Lemons."

Lemon Tart

Use Oatmeal pie crust recipe on page 47. Add Lemon Custard   .

Melt in top of double boiler 1/4 pound butter adding 1 1/2 cups of Xylitol or stevia. Add grated rind of organic lemons. Omit rinds, if you can't find organic lemons. This will have less familiar flavor without grated rinds, but due to the use of fungicides on lemons today in some orchards this minimizes potential of adding chemicals to your diet.

Squeeze 3 lemons and add juice to butter.

Once butter is melted, remove from stove and whip into the mixture 6 organic eggs.

Stir well. Cook in double boiler over hot water until custard is thickened. About 20 minutes.

Pour mixture into the pie crust shells. Refrigerate. Enjoy when the urge to splurge nags you. Squeezed Lemon can also be added to salads as dressing instead of vinegar for a change of taste.

Tip: Squeezed Lemon can also be added... for a change of taste.

Vinegar and Amino Delights

Vinegar Benefits. Internal. They are:*Rich in enzymes. *Help to Maintain Enzymes & Potassium. *Help Maintain Vibrant Skin.*Natural Antibiotic * Promotes Youthful Energy and Body. Weight Management.*Helps Build Healthy Scalp// Lessens Dandruff *Improve Digestion * Soothe joints and muscles.*Help Remove Toxins

Vinegar as a food was popularized by Dr Paul Bragg and Dr. Patricia Bragg, health pioneers who founded the company, Health Science out of Santa Barbara, California. They emphasized healthy habits, sharing a lifestyle of Love, Joy, Health, Spiritual, Emotional and Physical aspects of the person in their book, <u>The Miracles of Apple Cider Vinegar</u>. In the book they describe the undistilled *Bragg Organic Apple Cider Vinegar* as a way to add to healthy food choices. The Bragg version of vinegar is in its natural state with malic acid (undistilled) from naturally fermented apple cider vinegar. Bragg also markets *Bragg Liquid Aminos* for added nutrition in salads and main dishes Both products can be found in health food stores and some grocery chains.

Bragg books and products can be ordered from:
Health Science. Box 7, Santa Barbara, CA 93102. USA or call: 1-805-968-1020.

Founder, Dr. Paul Bragg, died in his 90's from a surfing accident. Health Science can be called for questions and they still do seminars. Their website: <bragg. com> tells where these seminars take place and what health oriented books are available. Research on Vinegar has grown to over 11 books plus articles from <u>Reader's Digest</u>, the Bragg family books, <u>Prevention</u> and <u>Bottom Line.</u> Research is intense at universities like Stanford, Harvard and groups like Mayo Clinic. Patricia Bragg said in her book, <u>The Miracles of Apple Cider Vinegar Health System,</u> our health and well-being are at stake. The physical is only part of what gives us a rich life. The other part is spiritual. All of these habits can be used by God to strengthen us, but we choose our habits and attitudes. *What we do with our life can make a difference for us and for those we love.*

Vinegar Salad Dressing. Step 1. Wash greens in veggie wash. Dry greens in a towel before adding to salad bowl

Step 2. Coat greens with 2 tbsp. olive oil to help salad stay fresh.

Step 3. Cut a variety of vegetables such as shredded broccoli, radishes, tomatoes and others like shredded cauliflower or turnips.

Step. 4. Drizzle 1 tbsp. vinegar over salad and mix.

Step 5. Add 1/2 tsp. sea salt and 1 tbsp. agave nectar over salad.

Making your own Salad Dressing lends freshness and avoids additives. This can be fun as you try the different flavored vinegars. **Basic ingredients for dressings from your cupboard are:** 1 cup olive oil.1 tsp. sea salt.1 tsp. agave nectar.1 cup of vinegar.

Japanese Salad Dressing Variation. Use the vinegar dressing recipe above. Substitute sesame oil and rice wine vinegar.

See Also: For Slaw Surprise recipe, see Page 42.

Mid-day Snacks
Chapter 2

Enter As Strangers.

Leave As Friends.

Date-Nut Snack Bars

(This treat adds potassium, iron & calcium. It may be used as a breakfast bar or to curb the urge for less wholesome snacks. You may substitute Stevia, Splenda or honey or agave.

A. 1/2 cup melted butter

B. 1 cup agave or honey. Other Options are: If, Splenda, Stevia or other sugar substitute 1/8 to1/4 cup to taste.

C. 3 eggs. Mix above ingredients well.

D. Add: 1 cup oatmeal blended into flour like consistency.

E. 1 tsp. baking powder, 1/2 tsp. salt, 1 tsp. vanilla.

F. 1 cup dates & 1 cup nuts chopped in food processer. You may use nuts only or substitute Truvia or Stevia for agave to cut calories. Flavor will be that of less sweetness.

G. Some studies show that Splenda or Stevia is safer than Xylitol because of pollutants in the Xylitol, if it is imported from Russia. USA grown Xylitol does not appear to have these issues currently.

H. Bake in 14 X 8 inch pan at 350 degrees for 30 minutes until mixture is set. Cool. Cut into squares and serve. Splenda or Stevia are sweeteners listed in <u>Prevention Magazine's</u> book, <u>The Sugar Solution</u> by Sari Harrar, and in other nutrition books. These books are found in health food and grocery stores. It is advised that you consult a physician, if you have medical issues as this is not a substitute for medical advice.

Coconut Almond Nuggets

When you have the desire to have a candy bar, this small treat can curb the urge. The other variations give you the chance to tailor this to your own tastes. To begin, get a fresh coconut. Crack and remove outer hard shell with a hammer. With a pick, drill hole in two coconuts eyes and drain juice for later use. Peel off hard crust to leave the pure coconut (fine, brown coconut skin and inner white flesh). Place this in the food processor to create coconut flakes. Freeze what you do not use for later recipes.

Version 1. Coconut-Almond Granola Bits.

1. Place the following ingredients in food processor. 1/2 cup honey, 1/2 cup agave. (You may substitute 3/4 cup of sorbitol, Xylitol or other sweeteners such as organic cane sugar. If using dried sweeteners, add 1/2 cup of coconut milk to moisten. Add: 1 cup ground almonds, 1/2 tsp. salt (optional). The more that we minimize cane sugars, the healthier our cells will probably be. (See: Pages 6 & 7).

2. Add: 1 cup ground granola (See: LeRoy's Breakfast Granola recipe. Page 10.)

3. Mix in blender until consistency of a candy bar. Form into small quarter sized balls. 4. Place on a cookie sheet coated first with olive oil. Freeze. When hardened, remove and place in container or box for future nibbles.

Version 2. Chocolate Dipped Granola Bars

1. Use 4 cups ground coconut. 2 cups granola. 1 cup Xylitol or stevia. 1 cup coconut milk. 1/2 cup barley flour, 1 cup whey, 1 cup finely ground almonds.

When mixture is blended to consistency of a cake before baking, place the mixture in 8 x 14 glass baking pan. Put in freezer for 30 minutes to harden batter. Cut into 2 x 6 inch bars. Remove to cutting board. Dip each bar into chocolate sauce. (See: Page 45 for Good 4 U Chocolate Sauce). Store in freezer in eco-friendly glass container.

Version 3. Chocolate Cherry Bars.

To the Version 1 above, add 1 cup of diced frozen cherries.

Diet Tips.

30 minutes exercise, distilled water. Review plan with your doctor. Know Fat burning foods. Avoid commercially processed foods, fake butters. Read labels.

Know foods that prevent fat burning ie. Use raw foods, when possible.

Cut or eliminate sugar, orange juice, "junk" processed foods, muffins, canola oils, fake butters, margarines or hydrolyzed oils.

Eat whole grain or gluten free breads & organic cereals.

No soy, sweeteners or corn syrups or minimize them.

Emphasize fruits, vegetables, lean organic meats, poultry and fish. Orange, green & red vegetables also can help as a base for your plan.

Don't shop when hungry. Keeps choices leaner. Read labels.

Keep a food diary. Read labels on food supplements and check with doctor who understands nutrition about your daily requirements.

If children or others in family need to lose weight, engage them in the challenge with a weekly reward when they see weight go down. Monitor progress with positive reinforcements. Check out books: The Power of Encouragement by David Jeremiah, The Language of Love Focus on the Family Publishing Co., by Gary Smalley and John Trent. Lifetime Conversation Guide, Prentice Hall Publishing Co., by James Van Fleet. The Country Doctor Handbook by editors of FC&A Publishing Co. Keeping a positive attitude goes a long way for some in this challenge.

Help bones with regular exercise. Keep a journal.

Check levels of fat in diet and monitor, but do not eliminate fats, except as ordered by your doctor. Substitutes for fats suggested are: apple sauce, pureed prunes or paw paw fruit puree.

Filling fiber helps some people. Some breads feature organic, whole grains, nuts & seeds. One slice might help cut urge to splurge.

Make greens, fruits and veggies a steady base in your diet.

Cut down on salt, if you have heavy use of that salt shaker.

Chapter 3

The Lunch Bunch

Sails
Triangles pin hopes to sky,
Reach toward gull to lure me
Across the slip to open water.

Creaking dock dares me follow halyards
that stencil banner against the night.

"Take me with you," I whisper.
Entering within, I move out.
Sheeting blows taut. Boat rocks free.
We move on to deeper seas.--by Susan Anderson Coons.
As published in an anthology of writers, poets and artists. *In a Nutshell.* Hibiscus
Press. 1976

*Tip: The challenge: Find fellow adventures where you encourage each other in this
journey of health and wellness. We only travel this way once, so let's make the
most of it.*

Cathy Mann's Refrigerator Pickles

7 medium cucumbers sliced.

2 medium sweet onions sliced

1 cup chopped green pepper or one cup red pepper.

1 cup Bragg's apple cider vinegar

1 tbsp. pickling salt or sea salt

1 tbsp. each celery seed and mustard seed.

2 cups of agave, stevia, Nutria or other sugar substitute.

The traditional recipe calls for plain sugar and adds a load of sugar to the meal. The agave is still a sugar load, but is more healthful than plain sugar. The key is to avoid those sugars found to be harmful. It is to your advantage to read the journals listed in this book and others as they research the power of using the right foods in your menu.

Knowledge is power. You must get it. Then, use it.

Now: Mix cucumbers and salt and let stand 1/2 hour. Drain. Stir into this, peppers and onions. Mix remaining ingredients and pour over peppers and other vegetables. Refrigerate. This keeps for 3 months. Grated cabbage also works well in this combination as does adding both green and red peppers for color to the meal.

Wheat Alternatives

Allergies or suspected sensitivities can be a challenge, but can sometimes be helped when we watch what we eat and the environment. For some, wheat, corn and dairy are sensitivities. This can often be tracked by a food journal as part of the sleuthing. For some people, allergies change the brain cell patterns so that they may have cravings that cause a weight gain or other health issues. In such cases, overeating may not be a lack of will power, but a brain cell deficiency. When improved, those people make healthier choices more easily.

One example of this trigger can come from some wheat or grains we might unknowingly be eating to which we are allergic. Some bakeries use organic grains, but others use chemically treated grains for a longer shelf life. Here are foods that might help. Check with a physician to see if they are right for you. Clam chowder, Vegetable soup. (Ask cook or chef if wheat is used,) Shrimp, Chicken & Fish Stir Fried at Chinese Restaurant. Is MSG used? Some people are allergic to shrimp also. Chicken dishes without batter. Vegetarian Dishes. Bouillabaisse, Ratatouille, Minestrone, Mussels. Check to see if they are breaded. Bean and lentil soups. Many fishes are good. Stay high in vegetables & low in additives. Fruit desserts. i.e., some restaurants serve cantaloupe, or grapefruit for dessert. If not on menu, ask if they can serve it, anyway.

This Song All Rich in Vibrato.
Reflections at a Concert in Anchorage, Alaska

This vibrato rich symphony calls to us as we enter the concert hall passing those hungry ones on the steps of the building. Memories of other concerts urge us to seek beauty in all areas of life. Waiting, we remember that healing touch of Christ as a source of completion over the years. We look forward to music that will carry us beyond primal longings for shelter and food to more sweet desserts like the ones enjoyed earlier that evening. Waiting for the concert to begin, we look beyond the panoramic window. An eagle glides towards its nest on a cliff.

The conductor and orchestra test instruments as we follow the eagle's flight. As it finds salmon, the eagle hovers, gathers food, and carries it to its nest. In counterpoint, musicians warm instruments, reminding us that this is a place of renewal. The conductor with violins, oboes, drums promise divine melody-- once they finish tuning. Deep inside of our being, we sense that we also can reach for grace notes. We listen as the Master Conductor brings order from cacophony. He replaces chaos with beauty that we might not have known had we not attended.

The Conductor raises His baton. He dips. He releases into the arena. A graceful waltz in 3/4 time. We bow to the Master's creation. The music's clear bell tones offer restoration. We lean back into our seats. From this beginning, heavenly chords pour symphony into our own being.

We learn to enjoy skipped notes as The Master teaches us to rescue lives.

Counterpoint from off-beat strophes lend richness to our own life music. As the toccata and fugue touch us, we remember some that we might miss in the rush of life. In our minds' ear, we hear the wails of fragile beings who cry in the streets of life. We think now of ways to understand their pain, their own hungry search. We wrap them in our hearts and spirits and take up our own instrument. We ask Almighty how we might share the larger sound. He lifts his baton again as we harmonize with another stroke from The Master Violinist.

The Prelude ends. Toccata and Fugue begin.

Tip: Stop and smell the roses and add to the music, when you can.

Avocado Mayonnaise Substitute for Salad Dressing.

1. 1 avocado. Beat until thick.

2. Add 1/2 tsp. mustard. 1 tsp. paprika.

3. 1/2 tsp. salt.

4. 1 tsp. agave nectar or replace agave with Stevia, if needed.

5. 2 tbsp. Braggs Apple Cider Vinegar or equivalent.

6. Add 1 cup olive oil.

Directions: Blend in blender until smooth. Once blended, this may be substituted for mayonnaise.

Tips: A. Can be doubled once you try it and like it. Using this will give you more Alpha lipoic acid and oils needed for wholesome energy sources.

B. You can also try a paste from the inside of the avocado rind and a bit of the mash leftover. Apply that to your face, when no one is looking. Rinse off and see if it helps with wrinkles, etc. Use this for one month and decide. Organic. Free use of leftover rind. Worth the try?

French or Japanese Salad Dressing. Making salads fun

Plan A. French Dressing

1. 1/2 cup olive oil, 2 tbsp. apple cider vinegar, and 1 tsp. salt.

2. 1/2 tsp. freshly ground black pepper. You can be creative and use other favorite herbs grown on your kitchen window sill or other place in house during the winter.

3. 1 tsp. agave nectar or honey.

Step One: Place mixture in blender and mix until smooth. For salad base use organic greens and grate into mixture carrots, cabbage, broccoli, and any other vegetables that you might grate that are available. Tomatoes are a good addition, but they do better if added to salad at last minute without putting them into the refrigerator.

Step Two. Coat salad blend with olive oil before adding the new salad dressing. The oil coating makes the salad stay fresher longer and brings out the best flavors of the vegetables. The agave, if available, gives that salad a twist that makes some persnickety nibblers take another bite.

Plan B. Japanese Dressing. Explore Exotic Japanese Flavors.

1. Substitute the olive oil with sesame oil.

2. Use rice vinegar instead of cider vinegar.

3. Add water cress and other light greens like butter lettuce to get the flavors of your favorite Japanese restaurant. You can also add your own sprouts, parsley, clove of garlic to marinate in the bottle. Yumm.

Chapter 4

Dinner
Sewing Tales of the Day into One Gift.

We gather at the table, share our yarns of the day. We weave them into one bright tapestry, to mend broken hearts, stitch caring memories. Our souls reach out to those we love in bonds that transcend daily concerns through this meal and with the power of encouragement. We bow our heads and honor the Great Provider, knowing that we can be glad for the day. For those times when we might be unsure, we sew and cook anyway, releasing memories to bind us to each other. We choose to live with faith and love for a finer warp and woof of life's garment and the tastier meal in a healing community as the gift.

Tip: In the Philippines honey is used to boost immunity for children. It is called "Tiki-Tiki" and is given to young children as a vitamin drink.

Know Your Sources.

Get to know your local farmers and/or fishermen. Find out what pollutants might be in the foods that you consume. There are several ways to uncover this valuable information.

1. Shop local Farmer's Markets. Get to know the farmers and/or fishermen. As you become a regular buyer, they'll be glad to see you.

Ask questions, when you know the rancher/farmer.

A. How do you raise your "Corn"? Peas? Beans?

B. Which of these do you like the best?

C. Do you use preservatives to keep your food fresh? What are they?

D. How long will this bag of veggies//fruit stay fresh?

E. May I come to your farm for a day of harvesting?

Some ranches feature "You Pick Days" in order to increase sales. This offers a great Saturday outing for you, your family and friends. You can pick enough for the freezer for next winter at the same time.

F. Where do you get the fish? Raise your beef? Lamb? Chicken? Is it local? Is it a better buy in bulk?

2. When you shop at large chain store grocers, ask questions of produce and meat department managers. Often, they know that those with questions might shop often, if satisfied. When you win, so do they.

3. There are a variety of co-ops to which you can belong. I actually received a dividend check of $18.00 from a co-op where I shop. This was based on the amount spent at that organic food store in the past year. That store plus the weekly farmer's market are two resources where many "buy locally" to support the ranchers and merchants of the area.

Know Your Sources (Continued)

     A. Questions to ask. Where were these carrots//beans grown? I did this at two local grocery stores and added that I wanted to buy USA, organic, preferably, locally. Signs in both organic sections now show produce grown in USA plus labels on fruits and vegetables marked "Certified Organic." Others probably asked also and I shop those two stores now on a regular basis along with the local "Farmer's Market."

     B. Shop sales to save dollars. Collect small, orphaned jars with lids to store excess tomatoes, etc. for later use. A label on jars with a date helps so that your freezer isn't a bunch of outdated, old food. Then, rotate. Making a chart of this can be helpful.

     C. Become a label and a health journal reader. <u>Newsmax</u> is a journal that comes in the mail or online. IVL also has a journal that helps. They tell about how to manage nutrition, preparation, supplement knowledge and food selections. You can also learn much about nutrition on websites, such as: <u>Newsmax, Health Science Institute Newsletter, Mayo Clinic Newsletter</u> and its book, as well as <u>Reader's Digest book, Foods That Harm, Foods That Heal.</u>" As you sleuth, you will find other sites, books and magazines. Remember that anyone can say anything on the internet, so use discernment. "Knowledge is Power." Sherlock Holmes has nothing on you, since you have more resources than he did.

     D. If you can afford the time, local health food stores and Adult Education Extension classes offer a wealth of valuable seminars. County Extension Agencies also offer classes on how to raise vegetables, etc.

     E. Sleuth local organic grains, cereals and breads to increase your bank of information. Even grocery chains have been bitten by the "organic bug."

     F. Find friends who like to garden. In a low key way you and they can share ideas on ways to make this project work for all of you. Neighbors can even swap vegetables when in excess. See also the section on Page 64. "Container Gardens in Unlikely Spots."

     G. Garden club members often share information for a good use of your/their time.

     H. Consider taking part of this project to your local school, helping a teacher as an "aide" with a unit on "Grow Your Own Garden" in pots in the room or helping with a plot outside. Keeping the project in the classroom limits the temptation of other classroom rabbits from nibbling your student's lettuce. The teacher can blend this into his/her ecology unit, etc. You could learn from her or him as well, and gain valuable back-up of having the parent's consent for this project. As a former fifth grade and high school teacher, I urge you to take the step of working as a parent, teacher or community resource to make this fun as you share it with others.

Home Made Frozen Yogurt Ice Cream

This recipe is easy and tasty. It uses fruits on hand that have been frozen in advance and makes an alternative to commercial ice cream. Try it! If your guests and family like it, you have a nutritional winner. So far, I have only heard good reports, even though this is not your conventional "ice cream."

Freeze organic peaches, strawberries, blueberries or whatever organic fruit is available in your area. Also collect organic bananas and freeze them with the skins on in freezer. You'll find more uses for those frozen bananas once you try them. They keep in the freezer for about 6 months. *Xylitol is a new sweetener with mixed reports about its nutritive value. The North and South American variety comes from birch instead of the corn syrup of Russian brand is reported to be more wholesome by some labs.* Take 2 cups frozen fruit. Add 2 bananas cut into 2 inch slices with skins removed by running under water before peeling away the banana skins.

Thaw fruit and cut into 1 inch pieces small enough for blender.

Add 1 cup frozen yogurt.

Add 1/2 cup Splenda, Nutria, Xylitol or other non-sugar, low calorie sweetener. Add 1/2 cup agave syrup, unless diabetic. If diabetic, increase the sugar substitute, but research Resources. **Page 65**, and/or use your own sources. Some sweeteners have shown negative lab reports. The ones reported under **Sweeteners, on Page 44,** had favorable ratings. Building awareness is a key to good health. Only you can decide that this is a vital part of your life journey.

Pour mixture into bottom of blender with 1/2 cup organic cow or goat milk to help with the blending process.

Once this mixture is blended, pour it into 1 cup dishes or containers. Return the sorbet to your freezer for partial hardening for about 1/2 hour. This gives a creamy sorbet or sherbet and cuts the amount of additives for your diet compared to those in commercial ice creams or sherbets. Now you are ready for a dessert that is good for you

Keeping Breaks and Dinners Lean and Fun.

If you have attended workshops recently, you may have noticed the number of people who bring their own water bottles or pick up a bottle of commercial water in a plastic container. For those concerned about the environment and health, it is comforting to know that you can bring your own water container to these events. Then you cut down on the contaminants found in some commercially bottled water products. Mannatech, Multipure and other companies now make available sturdy water jugs that are easily carried with you. A bonus is that you fill the thermos with a source of water from your own water filtration system. Besides carrot sticks and apples, one way to feel full between meals is to use this seminar break time to work in the 8 glasses of water that doctors and health groups so tout as critical for good health. Two ideas here can also fill in for dinners:

1. Avocado-Mayonnaise salad dressing on page 28

2. Involve family members, even young children in this health promoting project. You might form the Smith Family Get Up and Go Stronger Association. Your children can be on your Board of Directors with a monthly meeting that ends in a healthy treat. Keeping a light touch to your wellness adventure can make it fun for others. A sign on a local taxi cab says this well. "Just say no to foods on drugs." They share ideas on how to make this fun and still work. One can be Secretary and take notes. The Sergeant of Arms keeps track on a chart of who did what, last month in their own wellness and gardening projects. They might be part of your kitchen gardener project. The increased awareness can help all in the household live a healthier life.

Keeping Dinners Lean and Fun. (Continued)

One idea that helps in some households is for each person to have their own pitcher that holds 8 glasses of water. Label it for that person. If in a family, let a "Sergeant of Arms" keep track of who reaches their 8 Glasses Goal each day. Some of the water can be drunk between meals instead of harmful sodas and chemically loaded fast foods. One selling point might be the better energy gained than if their body is loaded with harmful sugars that end in "ose."

With this committee approach, children gain status within the family structure. If no children or other people are involved, you can use a simple tracking system for yourself, knowing that you are cleaning sludge that slows others down. At the end of the first month, review goals with points for Mission Accomplished. Then, celebrate!

Dinner might be a time to do a review of how "Members of the Board" did with their Healthy Directions Goal for the Day. Keep the atmosphere friendly on this one. When my children were in elementary school, I didn't know to take this step. As a result, I spent time and money looking for gluten free sources and baking "healthy" foods. Later, when an adult, my daughter shared that she loved spending time with one friend, who supplied her with a nice dose of junk food daily. The more we engage our family, the better the chance for success. Drinks can be: apple, mango, lemonade, pomegranate juice. Goat milk, rice milk can be alternatives, if milk allergies are a problem. Check grocery store for certified organic milk, if you prefer the traditional beverage. Reader's Digest and Prevention Magazine, and Chinese, Japanese cookbooks can lend ideas to this project.

Alfalfa Sprouts in a Jar or Dish

1. **1 or 2 quart jar** with strainer top of fine wire screen or cheesecloth anchored by the outer ring of a lid.

2. 1 tsp. sprouts for 1 quart jar or 1 tsp. sprouts for 2 quart jar.

3. Soak seeds overnight in jar with enough purified water to cover.

4. In the morning, drain off excess water being certain strainer is secure. Always use lukewarm water for this process.

5. Put jar on side. Jiggle seeds to the side of jar on kitchen counter.

6. Rinse seeds twice a day through strainer top.

7. Leave strainer top on throughout sprouting process. Avoid direct sunlight, but keep in light area.

When sprouts show 2 fully opened green leaves, they are ready for use. This usually takes 4-6 days. Rinse, Drain and store in airtight container in refrigerator. Use as soon as possible. +++ ++++++

37

Alfalfa Sprouts in a Dish. Or other sprouts. This same sprouting process can happen by placing seeds in a dish.

Use same light and rinsing conditions as above. Cover with 6 layers of cheese cloth. Terry cloth may also be used, but cheese cloth works best. This takes about the same 4-6 days.

Rinse again with lukewarm water. When most sprouts show 2 leaves, rinse, drain and store in refrigerator. Use as soon as you can.

Good to sprinkle over omelets or in stir fry dishes. The type of seeds used will result in different sprouts.

Hagendorf Hash.
(Good for stuffing turkey or fish.)

In a stir fry pan for stir fry or glass baking dish: Place.
1. 1 large sweet onions diced.

2. 1/2 red onion diced.

3. 4 cups cooked brown or wild rice.

4. 1 red pepper diced.

5. 1 large portabella or other mushrooms diced.

6. 4 oz. dried cranberries.

7. 3/4 tsp. grated black pepper.

8. 1 tsp. salt or to taste.

9. 1/2 cup butter or 1/2 cup olive oil.

10. 1 cup chicken or turkey broth. (See recipe p. 57).

11. 1 tsp. Italian seasoning, oregano, marjoram, ground bay leaf, or herbs from your kitchen garden.

This can be a stir fry vegetable dish or can be baked in glass baking dish until thermometer shows 165 degrees.

If using this to stuff a turkey, add 1 cup of organic sunflower seed bread or another favorite of yours.

Old Family recipe from the Hagendorf/Hawkins Clan.

Tip: Be a label reader before you buy. I picked up a favorite Greek yogurt and discovered that the company now adds fructose, a form of sugar and corn syrup.

Lavender Splash

Susan had a still for her lavender *brew*
There she made a gallon or two.
The birds got a whiff of the fumes from the stew.
They stopped their flying, practiced napping...then celebrated this new brew.

What to do with *Lavender Splash?*
1. Spritz on pillow for a restful sleep.
2. Spritz in cupboards to discourage moths.
3. Spritz in kitchen and bathroom for Fragrant refresher.
4. Use in <u>Crème Brule</u> as replacement for part of the cream. For one recipe, you can replace up to 1/4 cup cream and save a few calories. Less rich tasting.
5. Use as after shave lotion or add to bath.
6. Squirt brew on your face. People will wonder what spa you have been visiting.
7. Lavender once brewed keeps best in refrigerator.
8. According to more than one person this has helped them to relax as it is soothing.
9. Lavender grows in many climates and pots. Fun to grow.

Note: Lavender grains may be turned to splash by simmering them in water for two hours. Use one packet of lavender seeds per three quarts of water. Boil until brew turns brown. Lavender was brought in a packet on a trip, because of limits on plane.

Urge to Splurge Chocolate Drops

1 four once Ghirardelli "Natural" or Hershey's dark chocolate baking bar.

1/4 cube organic butter plus 2 tbsp. coconut oil.

1/4 cup honey, 1/4 cup Stevia in the Raw, 1/2 cup raw turbinado sugar.

(Can use all stevia for sweeteners, but it is bitter for some people. Also: Can substitute all raw turbinado organic sugar. Found at some grocery stores in a package, or in bulk at some health food stores.)

1 cup oatmeal

1/8 cup flax seeds, 1/2 cup sunflower seeds, 1/2 cup dried cranberries

1 tsp. vanilla, 1/2 cup organic apple juice. Read labels. This juice is now in some stores.

Step One: Melt Chocolate bar, honey, butter, coconut oil. Once melted, add Stevia and turbinado sugar. Or, all sugar, if you prefer the taste. Stevia saves calories and challenges that some people have with regular sugar.

Step Two: When the above is melted on stove, add oatmeal and cook until oats are blended into mixture. (*About 3 minutes)

Step Three: Add vanilla, flax seeds, sunflower seeds, and cranberries, vanilla. Mix well.

Step Four: Allow mixture to cool enough to form into quarter size balls by rolling in palm of your hands. Cool 1/2 hr. in refrigerator. Gooey, but worth the work. These drops are rich, so one or two drops make a dessert or treat. Can be stored later in refrigerator. Addictive for some. You might keep them... out of easy reach, but still available enough to enjoy when the urge to splurge hits you or others.

Journey of the Soul-- Headed for Heaven

Based on one person's journey with God.

Eternity calls! Its sun in orbit whispers of God's glorious universe, while we search for answers to life in those billions of galaxies. From our cubicle…even the stars seem mute at first.

Yet, a reminder of His Cross abides in that planetary terrain that shines across ages and rests with us even as we watch night skies. Other clans of seekers hoping for answers scan their own Microsphere as that hunger for the Call of the Cross wells within them. Deep inside in spite of challenges faced, we sense that Christ is still at the core of our universe and does all things well. Knowing a bit of who He is keeps us awake at night. We try to understand why such an Almighty Adonai would care about our concerns, when so much in His universe demands attention. Questions pound at us like reverberations of stars traversing Galaxies. As the rays of the stars reach this moonstar called Earth, we set aside our wonder for a moment. A deep peace releases us to sweet sleep. We remember that one day Jesus Christ, Son of the Living God, will return in glory to reclaim the next chapter of this book called, Eternity. Knowing this, we can live in even deeper peace……grateful to know where we are headed.

LeRoy's Wow 'Em Salad.

Step One. Gather the veggies. Step Two: Think outside of the box.
Start with organic greens. This base is key.

Add any raw vegetables that can be sliced and grated. The fresher and more organic, the better the flavor seems to be.

Suggestions: Grated radishes, carrots, cabbage, anise leaves or anise root. Sliced celery, diced jicama, peas, beans, red pimento, green peppers, and snow peas. Grated beets. Sweet potatoes or red potatoes grated. This gives a salad that is flavorful and colorful

Sliced green onions, cucumbers or basil. Sometimes, people cannot digest some choices. If so, you might serve them in separate dishes.

Sunflower seeds or other nuts.

Wash all vegetables with an organic vegetable wash. Roll in a towel while assembling the salad dressing.

Step Two. Salad Dressing, The star of the salad. Coat two tablespoons of olive oil over the greens once they are assembled before adding the salad dressing. This helps the salad to stay fresher longer. Then. Mix 1/4 cup of apple cider vinegar, 1/2 cup olive oil, 2 tbsp. of pure agave nectar sweetener with salt and pepper to taste. Pour this carefully over salad until taste is right for you.

An alternative for dressing is: sesame oil with rice vinegar and agave syrup in the same proportions as #7. This adds occasional variety to the salad and might become a favorite part of the meal from reports received.

To vary: Add chicken, tuna or other meats for a "fast food" meal. Also, you can use leftovers stuffed into a burrito wrap as a lunch on the road.

Check the flowers listed under edible flowers and wash carefully with a veggie wash. You just might see salads as a new adventure. One family makes it a challenge to see how much they can get into their salad that they never tried before using LeRoy's Wow 'Em Salad Dressing.

Salmon /Halibut Delight

What do you do with fish? Tip: Alaskan fishermen have ways of preparing halibut and salmon. This recipe can be adapted to any fish, even when you have fish from the freezer where you want to revive it to freshly caught zest. Follow these steps and judge for yourself. This is based on what Margaret Coons, a teacher in Kodiak, Alaska, shared what some fishermen in that area do with their fish for a tasty change.

1.While preparing and sautéing the vegetables, soak 2 pounds of cleaned fish in 1/2 cup milk plus the juice of one lemon .

2. Slice into slivers: one sweet white onion, one red pepper, one green bell pepper, one yellow pepper, 1/2 cup fresh dill.(Dill can be grown in a kitchen pot, if you can't find it in stores.) 1 cup slivered zucchini, 1/2 cup parsley, 1/2 cup celery, 1 tbsp. garlic, 1/2 cup slivered onions, 2 medium tomatoes diced. 4 mushrooms sliced.

3. Sauté' slivered vegetables in 2 tbsp. butter plus 2 tbsp. olive oil. For added flavor, add 1 tsp. tarragon or Oregano to taste.

4. Remove fish from milk. Bake in oven at 350 degrees. Add 1/2 cup of cream and 1/2 cup sweet white wine, like moscato or sherry for about 15 minutes until fish starts to flake with fork. (Cream gives this a richer flavor). For last five minutes of baking, cover with sautéed vegetables.

5. Serve with wild rice, brown rice. Some people barbecue the fish and then add the vegetables over the top on serving. This serves four people.

Tip: Leftovers can be used for tortillas or Japanese "spring rolls" as a next day meal. To maintain freshness, refrigerate cooked fish at end of meal.

Weeds
(Ways to fight weeds.)

Yellow dandelions of gossip bloom.

Then they spread seeds across our lawns, unless removed before they turn to feathery sprouts.

Grasses out of place pop up in our rose garden like unforgiveness, infesting corners of the mind's landscape when least expected.

That ivy of haughty condemnation travels below the surface and climbs a favorite bush to choke growth in vine-like undertones.

It dares us find its vast underground root system where tendrils hide.

How much less painful might it be to pull the first leading of these Tyrants of the Soul and nip them......................before they bud.

Getting Rid of Weeds without sprays.

1. On lawns spread lime

2. Carry a small knife when on lawn. Dig up dandelions and other weeds when they are small and the ground is still moist. At first this will be work, but once the lawn is cleared, you'll be glad that you did. It works for some!

3. Do you have other Ideas? Send to Coons-Hawkins @ P.O. 927. North Bend, OR 97459. We might use them in a second edition and you can help others. *"True Friends are like angels. You don't have to see them, to know they are there."*

Sweeteners

One thing to consider when choosing sweeteners is that the more that we cut back on the use of those sugars shown to be harmful, the better our odds are for good health. Is this a guarantee? No. Each person's body is unique. Those who test as hypoglycemic or diabetic do well to avoid the sugars that cause energy or sugar problems. Some sugar substitutes are not yet fully tested and certified by the FDA. There are now so many different sweeteners that the question arises, "What are the hidden sugars contained in some foods? This brief review will not give answers to all of these questions, but it might cause you to search for your own answers. Oh, So Delicious! And Healthy, Too! Cookbook Will be updated later with comments from friends & critics willing to share. To begin-- here are a few ideas from sources such as books and magazines. Those with medical issues from allergies or sugar problems should check with their physician.

1. Stevia Extract is a 0 calorie *plant based sweetener that* can be obtained from a company called, "Sugar in the Raw." One tester said it has a stronger taste than other sugar substitutes. It comes from the foliage of the Stevia plant grown in South America for 400 years and has been used in Japan for over 40 years.

2. Xylitol is another plant based 0 calorie sweetener that has come out in markets in bulk. One company sells it under the name of Truvia. It contains 0 calories with erithritol and rebiona. Xylitol is grown in two main places, Russia and South America. The Russian version has been downgraded by the FDA due to pollutants. There is a concern that it might cause cancer. Similar or other questions have been raised for aspartame, saccharin and several other sweeteners.

4. Agave is extracted from the agave cactus like plant which is more like honey in structure than other substitutes. It is considered by many to be good for you, but is still a form of sugar.

5. White cane, raw cane sugar & brown sugar are traditional sweeteners and often cause problems for diabetics or hypoglycemic.

Good 4-U Chocolate Sauce

1/2 Cup Hershey's Chocolate powder or other powdered chocolate
1 stick organic butter
1/2 cup Xylitol, Stevia, Nutria or Agave syrup (Check source, if Xylitol)
3/4 cup organic yogurt
1 tsp. vanilla

1. Melt butter on stove top.
2. Add yogurt, agave, Xylitol or other sugar substitute.
3. Once blended, add vanilla and cook until smooth. Use wire whisk to keep mixture smooth. If mixture has lumps or is too runny, put into blender with arrowroot powder and cook again using wire whisk.

This sauce is good over the fruit sherbets and frozen yogurts described elsewhere.

Lifestyle shift for household: Sweeteners for cooking: Fructose, Xylitol, stevia, honey, agave. Remember that American Xylitol made with birch is considered cleaner than Russian Xylitol which was tested to contain contaminants. If you get this Xylitol sweetener from a health food department of a chain or in a health food store, check to see what their source is. If in doubt, use one of the other sweeteners.

This is a new enough source of sweetener that it is not in some dictionaries.

Oatmeal/Bran/Rye Bread

1. Pour two cups boiling water over 1 cup organic, rolled oats in large bowl. Stir well. Let it stand 1hour. Instead of oats, you may use: 1 cup of other organic grains like bran or rye. Add the following:
2. 1/ 2 cup honey or 1/ 3 cup xylitol.
3. 2 tsp salt.
4. 1 tbsp butter or coconut butter, if dairy sensitive.
5. In small bowl, pour 1/ 2 cup lukewarm, purified water over 1 package of yeast. Let this sit until dissolved and foaming as yeast activates. Mix the above ingredients in the large bowl.
6. Add to the above: 4 1/2 cups organic oatmeal, barley, or organic wheat. Use gluten free wheat, if gluten intolerant.
7. Combine above. Let batter rise at room temperature until batter doubles. Form two loaves and place in bread pans. Bake at 250 degrees until bread is cooked about 40 to 50 minutes.

Tips: A. *Once batter has risen, added pecans or walnuts with 1 cup raisins makes a satisfying breakfast loaf.*

B. *Hot or Spicey bread can be made of this base with a favorite spice, such as chiles or coriander.*

C. *If you bite into food that is too hot, dip bread into olive oil to take away some of the heat, according to the Flour Lady.*

D. *The Joy that you give to others is the Joy that comes back to you.*

E. *Some people are allergic to bran or oats, if bread contains gluten. If this is the case, ask your health food store for gluten free oats. Also, try oat flour without wheat to see if you enjoy the flavor.*

(My tasters liked it.)

Oatmeal Pie Crust Hmmmm

Makes enough for one pie, top & bottom; or two single crusted pies.

Grind two cups oat flour in blender until powdered consistency.
1 tsp. salt
2/3 cup butter softened. (Alternative =1/3 cup coconut and 1/3 cup butter)
Mix the above in a mixmaster until blended. Do not overbeat as that makes crust tough. Wrap dough in wax paper and chill. Another option is to wrap into paper towel and then into wax paper to keep a distance between dough and wax paper.

Once well chilled, divide crust into two parts. Roll each part into a ball. If you want one single crust pie, the other part can be frozen once rolled into pie crust shape and placed in pie pan.

Tip: One unusual use for flour was shared by a friend. She calls herself the "flour lady" and keeps a pan of flour in her freezer for mild burns. If someone in her household gets a burn, she covers that burned area with cold flour to neutralize the burn, unless it is serious enough for a doctor's visit. Then, she gets them to the doctor ASAP. No guarantees are made that this will work for you, but I tried it with good results for myself.

Apple and Blueberry Pies.
(Other berry pies can be adapted to this recipe)

Apple Pie Filling

Slice 6-8 apples. Put into pie crust in pan.

Mix 2 Tbsp. butter, 1/4 tsp. salt, 1/3 cup sugar or agave with 1 tsp. cinnamon.

Blend mixture into apples.

Cover with second crust Make slots in crust for steam to escape.

Bake at 425 degrees for 30 minutes or until done. Test with fork. Other fruits can be used with agave or honey.

Blue Berry Pie Filling

Three cups blue berries.

2 Tbsp. gluten free flour.

3/4 cup powdered stevia substitute. Increase lemon

1 tbsp. butter, 1/2 tsp. salt

1 tbsp. lemon juice as above. 4 tsp. lemon juice, if use stevia.

Pour either filling into pie crust and bake in oven at 425 degrees for 45 minutes. Balancing health concerns and calories becomes a challenge. Offering wholesome deserts or treats can minimize the craving for foods that use sugars that create imbalances in your system. Dr. Julian Whitaker, M.D., in his book, Dr. Whitaker's Guide to Natural Healing states, "The immunity of Americans, particularly those with infections or chronic problems, including chronic fatigue, is unnecessarily compromised by amount of sugar added by the food industry to our foods." Goal = to cut down on sugar = better than doing nothing.

Tip: If you can't change the ballgame of health with your family's food favorites, switch the pitch. You might hit a home run and still slip in healthy foods.

Desserts and Breads Freed From Wheat or Gluten

Several nutritional companies offer products for those with wheat and/or dairy allergies. It would take another book and much testing, etc., to review all aspects of allergens. As Science uncovers more alternative options to working with wheat and gluten allergies, it is worth spending time doing more research if you have a puzzling condition. KNOWLEDGE IS POWER. The more that you know, the more that you might cooperate with your physician in an educated manner. This can possibly help to make this a fun adventure as you gain that vitality you desire. Even those who do not think that they have wheat allergies can enjoy a trade-off for wheat on occasion.

1. Berry Fruit Compote. 2 cups berries, 1 cup minced mango, 1/3 cup chopped almonds, 1 tsp. Glycogen protein powder from Mannatech or a comparable protein powder from the store. 1/4 cup soy, almond or rice milk or creamer. Gently mix fruit and then add creamer. Freeze until ready to eat. Some researchers suggest that protein mixes contain chemicals also. One writer suggests that you choose a diet with as many raw foods as you can and avoid stressing about what you might not easily change. Finding balance makes it better for some in the long run.

2. Chocolate Ice Cream. One ripe banana. 1 cup ground cashews.1 scoop powdered chocolate protein mix. 1 orange with seeds and rind removed. Put mixture in blender. Once blended, place in freezer until ready to serve. Take from freezer. Thaw slightly. Enjoy.

3. An alternative to the chocolate protein mix: Substitute 1 cup of yogurt, if no dairy allergies. Add vanilla protein mixed with frozen peaches, strawberries or other fruits for a variety of desserts that resemble a French sorbet in taste. The added frozen banana mixed in blender makes this creamier.

4. Plain Fruit as a dessert with <u>Good 4-u Chocolate Sauce,</u> on Page 45, dribbled over the top.
5. Lemon Tart. Page 18.

6. Coconut Almond Nuggets. Page 22.

7. Note: Some wheat is treated with ingredients that increase shelf life. This may decrease absorption of minerals in stomach. For that reason, some bakeries & health food stores offer "gluten free" breads. They may know which grains are less treated. If you have questions, check with physician and alternative medical resources.

**Tidbit: Prickly Pears, Nopalea, Kyani, Tumbleweed and Cactus.
Healthy Sources From Far Away Places.**

Tidbit: Cactus and its pears can be one source of food, if you are stranded in the desert. You can also find them at some larger supermarkets. Cactus juice known as prickly pear juice or Nopalea is a popular drink in many countries that is high in nutrients.

Tip: **Search the Internet for Sources, if you don't see it on your market shelves. Some companies have recipes to use the cactus juice or other juices.**

1. One company is Trivita with a juice called Nopalea. *You can order through Liz Welsh in Canada, who will tell you more about this product than space here permits. 1-780-483-8727.*

2. Another product where friends report help with energy and pain relief is **Kyani, a "Superjuice," which contains Wild Alaskan Blueberry, Pomegranate, Cranberry, Goji berry, Bee Pollen, Aloe Vera, Sockeye Salmon and more in its menu. This is something that the Tlingit tribe in Alaska have gathered from their land and used for many years with the benefit of an unusual healthy lifestyle. IF you try it, you'll know if it can also help you. For personal attention and questions answered, you can call pharmacist Dean Warner at 1-541-297-0345.** Mention this Oh, So Delicious Cookbook so that Dean knows to take more time with you, if you have questions.

Tumbleweed and Answers from Its Desert Refuge

Like explorers of other times from Abraham, Isaac, Paul--
The tumbleweed drifts across hills, rests briefly on a cactus.
With few roots to claim as its own, the cactus
offers no resistance to the tumbleweed,
but spreads its arms in shelter for the wanderer.
Nor does it question its existence
as it stands against desert heat in the midst of cactus neighbors.
Though the cactus offers few fruit and sparse shade,
we travelers still stop for a while,
finding relief and juice from the lean shelter
shaded from the fires of the day.
Refreshed then, we share life with those who pass our way.

Oatmeal Cookies

Ingredients:

1. 2 cups organic oatmeal. Blend in blender into fine powder. Place in mixing bowl.
2. Add: 1/2 cup organic oatmeal unground to mixture for texture.
3. Add: 1/2 cup Xylitol or Stevia sugar and add 1/4 cup agave syrup for more of the taste of sugar. To avoid all sugars, increase to 3/4 cup Xylitol or Stevia and eliminate agave. Stir above.
4. Add: 2 large organic eggs and 1 tsp vanilla.
5. 1/2 cup organic butter melted.
6. 1/2 cup organic yogurt.
7. Combine ingredients above in mixmaster.
8. Then add: 1 tsp baking powder, 1 tsp cinnamon, ½ tsp nutmeg. Blend well, but do not overbeat.
9. Add 1/2 cup cranberries or raisins with 1/2 cup slivered almonds or other nuts. The more that you cut or minimize sugars, the better for your health.
10. Preheat oven to 350 degrees. Coat two cookie sheets with non-stick spray.

Use Tablespoon to measure. Form mixture into flat round with palms of hands and place on cookie sheets. Bake 10-15 minutes until lightly brown. For an added touch, add a few cranberries or an organic pecan to cookie top.

Psalm 119:103: ". . . sweet are the words . . ."

Higher Protein Carrot/Vegetable Slaw

In food processer shred the following:

1. 4 carrots
2. 1 cucumber
3. 2 stalks celery
4. The stalk of 1 green onion
5. Leaf of red cabbage
6. 1/2 cup fresh peas
8. 1/2 cup Bermuda onion.
9 Now: Dice 1 red pimento.
10. Add. 1 cup garbanzo beans cooked and 2 cups wheat berries cooked. Use imagination and add other favorites.
11. Combine mixture in large bowl.
12. Add salad dressing. 1/2 cup olive. 1/4 cup rice wine vinegar. 1/2 cup cottage cheese. 1 tsp. minced chives & 1 tsp. parsley. 1 tsp. sea salt (Good idea to see if grocer or label can tell you where salt was harvested.)

The wheat berries and garbanzo beans can be cooked in bulk and used later in other dishes. This salad will keep for several days and can be added to leafy salad for variety. The grocer said that it is the wheat berries that increase protein, but it is not high protein like a meat dish.

Building Goodness Into Salads & Other Foods.

For many of you reading this modest sharing, you already are aware of the ideas about healthy eating and you practice these ideas in your daily meals. For that reason, I appreciate your indulgence in tidbits of information shared in this small booklet. My main purpose in writing this for all of us is to encourage that spirit of adventure when we see food differently. Shopping at a local supermarket that has a natural food section, I talked to the health food section manager. The information uncovered will influence how I shop.

1. The way that beef is raised makes a difference in the labels. The label "Organic" means no exposure to chemicals, antibiotics or growth hormones &animal or other foods are vegetarian fed. "Certified Organic" indicates laboratory testing for chemicals with none found. Organic usually costs more.

2. If labeled "Natural" that indicates that there are no antibiotics, hormones, nitrates in scheduled treatments and the food in question is always vegetarian fed. These animals and fruits and vegetables grow at their own pace in a reduced stress environment. Because the methods are less efficient, they might cost more. There might be sprays from a neighboring ranch that might on occasion drift into their environment, but these animals and other foods are fairly clean. This also affects foods in the fruit and vegetable sections. As the market manager suggested--No system will be a perfect system. However, we can be more ahead health wise than if we were to do nothing.

3. There is the added factor of the stress of trying to be perfect in this challenge. That can impose its own hazards to cells. We are learning about this in studies of the effects of stress on the body. In summary, the "all natural" label is different from the "organic" label. It helps for you to do some sleuthing. Discover how your favorite food was handled. That might make a difference for you and for those in your houehold.

Salsa

Salsa can be made of a variety of fruits and vegetables. The salsa most eaten is Tomato Salsa. From that basic idea, it is fun to play with this food by substituting peaches, mango, or other soft fruits or vegetables. This not a fixed dish. Common uses are with tortillas or meats, but I found recently that it also freshens fish and makes it seem more moist, when cooked on the stovetop.

1. Traditional Salsa. If you have a harvest of tomatoes, this can be made in quantity with the extra salsa frozen for winter. In food processor place the following and grind until it becomes like tomato slurry:

A. 3 cleaned tomatoes,

B.1 Walla Walla or other sweet onion --peeled,

C. 1 green pepper.

D. 1 papaya. Remove pulp from pit.

If you prefer a less mushy salsa, grate ingredients with a cheese grater on the finest side of grater. This takes more time.

E. Add: 2 tsp. fresh cilantro, if available, & 2 tsp. parsley. 1 tsp. salt. 1 tsp. dill. 1/2 tsp. pepper.1/2 tsp. oregano

F. 1 tsp. apple cider vinegar or rice wine vinegar.

G. 4 tbsp. olive oil

1 tbsp. agave. (This is a form of sugar but is optional. Some people add 3 tsp. wine or juice to mellow the salsa.)

Mix and store in jar in refrigerator. Avoid plastic or metal as tomato might leach some of these materials into the mixture.) Excess can be frozen.

Bouillabaisse

Bouillabaisse is a seafood dish from Southern France where the fishermen bring in a variety of fish and crayfish. Preparation takes time. I make a large pot and freeze 1/2 of portion for a later meal. "Exquisite," say some. "Worthy of a celebration," say others.

Step One. Make the Fish Stock below. In a large pot, place the following and simmer for 30 minutes.

1. 3 1/2 pounds of fish scraps: heads, tails, bones, pieces of large halibut that fishermen might normally discard1/2 cup celery diced.

2. Brown 2 mild onions in 1/4 cup olive oil.   1/2 tsp. salt to taste.

3. Add to 2 quarts of water in pot with 1 cup white wine & 1/2 cup sherry.

4. 3 cloves garlic, 1 bay leaf, 1/3 tsp. pepper.1/4 tsp. anise. 1 tsp. thyme.

5. When stock has simmered 20 minutes, strain broth.

Cool mixture. Discard bones. Go through mixture and pull out as many fish flakes and vegetables as you can without getting bones or skin in the mix. Throw away bones, and use leftovers by adding: oatmeal flour and eggs to bake into doggie cookies. You might be surprised at how dogs become a "good doggie" with this bribe. See recipe Page #60.What To Do With Leftovers.)

Step Two. Making the Bouillabaisse. Cut 2 pounds of halibut into 2 inch by 4 inch pieces. Add later when other ingredients are cooked and the flavor seems right. May add other whitefish also later for fresh taste.

2. Add 1 large jar, 16 ounces, of tomato ragu sauce and I jar Prego when available. Other brands are ok. 2 small cans tomato puree. 1/2 cup sherry.

3. Add 1 tsp. thyme, 3 fresh tomatoes cut into small pieces. 1 quart bottled clam juice from market. (About 2 jars.)

4. Add halibut and other fish from market or fish caught.

5. Add 12 steamed clams. 1 pint of mussels. 1 tsp. Anisette (French liquor). 1 pound of white fish like snapper. Add 1 lobster or crab broken into pieces so that the claws, etc., are divided, ready to be cracked with crab crackers. Add 1 pound of shrimp.

6. Serve with crackers, bibs, ample supply of big paper napkins and extra plates for shells. Finger bowl is a nice touch. Sourdough for dipping. Nice dessert is fruit with drizzle of chocolate sauce.   Bon Appetit!

Tip for all fish: If fish does not seem very fresh, soak for 1 hour in refrigerator with milk before cooking. Then, pour juice of one lemon over the fish before you cook it with 2 tbsp. of olive oil. This makes it fresher and more moist. If fish still smells too strong, you may wish to discard it.

Garlicky Chicken And Soup Broth

Stage One. Take one 4-5 pound organic chicken and cover with the following: 1/2 lemon, 1/2 cup olive oil. Drizzle olive oil and lemon over chicken. Flavor with 1 tsp. salt, 1 tsp. thyme, 1 bay leaf, 1/2 tsp. pepper.

Stuff cavity with brown rice flavored with 1 tsp. sage, 1 tsp. crushed bay leaf, 1 tsp. minced rosemary and 2 cloves minced garlic.

Stage Two. While chicken is baking in oven at 350 degrees, sauté 8 sliced crimini mushrooms in 2 tsp. olive oil plus 1/4 cup white wine (Optional). When lightly braised, set aside for final presentation.

Stage Three. When thermometer registers that chicken is cooked, slice and serve on platter with rice and mushrooms poured over the top. Serve for 4 people. Enjoy!

The next day…………………..

1. With leftover chicken, place bones, etc., in large pot.

2. Cover with filtered water.

3. Add 5 peeled, sliced carrots. 5 stalks celery. 1 large yellow onion. 3 cloves garlic. 1 tsp. salt & 1 tsp. pepper. 1 tsp. tarragon or sage to taste. 1 sprig parsley. 1 more bay leaf.

4. Simmer in pot for about 2 hours until meat falls off bones.

5. Remove chicken from broth. Chicken soup may be served with vegetables or put through strainer for broth only soup.

6. If broth only soup, you may add peas and bean noodles for Chinese style soup. The strained vegetables and skin, etc., are then good for Doggie Biscuits recipe on Page 60

7. You may suspect that this cookbook is about improvising as you adjust these recipes found in cookbooks to fit your needs. Part of the fun of cooking can be that of adapting a recipe to your dietary needs in such a way that limitations such as sugar or gluten free foods, are an adventure instead of a burden.

Hearty Barley Chicken Soup. Meal In A Pot Soup

6 cups organic chicken broth from page 56.

Simmer 1/2 cup each of barley & brown rice in pot. Cook until soft.

Add leftover chicken sliced to 1/4 inch thin strips. Vegetables from the broth made earlier can be saved for a casserole or added to this soup for even more flavor.

Add 1 cup mushrooms. Sprinkle over top of broth 1/4 cup minced parsley. Cooking time about 15 minutes.

For a Meal in a Pot on days when you are in a hurry, you can add the leftover slaw or salad from another day plus one cup of fresh or frozen green peas.

Grate parmesan or feta over the top for the final touch. This makes a quick meal with oatmeal cookies and fruit sorbet for dessert.

Chapter 5. The Rest of the Story
This New Sound

The chords of the organ haunt the air as concert goers look for ways to renew their spirits. "What child is this?" drifts across the theater, while one man dozes---perhaps exhausted by holiday shopping and festivities. Others wonder how they might bring life to family members who are visiting for the holidays.

Bold chords send blasts of "Joy to the World" across the room. They soothe our nerves as we cling to fresh hope for a new day. Then we join with the organist in "O, Holy Night" and claim those stars all brightly shining up above us around the perimeter of the room. We sing again with the others in the promise that we can "fall on our knees and hear angel voices."

We button up our overcoats as drums resonate with a ""Bahmm, bahmm" and the bells answer back, "ping, ping." The trombones and saxophones play a soft Silent Night; Deck the Halls, and Angels We Have Heard on High."

The "Ratatatat" and "Pim, Pim, Pim" of the drums and other instruments surround us with holiday music in a new sound. Our hearts grow warm again as we leave the concert hall with a clearer Hope for Tomorrow.

We remember that Jesus Christ is still alive and that He cares for us as much now as He did when he came to earth 2000 years ago. We ask ourselves what we might do to spread that love during all seasons.

The Treasure of Stir Fry

Tip: Another way to add freshness to a meal is by using tips from Oriental cuisine in their stir fry cooking. Called by one restaurant, "Mongolian Grill", this has been one place where one needs to pay close attention to preparation and to watch, while cooking, to keep this lightly cooked. Having the brown rice ready before beginning, the table set, and all vegetables sliced before the stir fry begins helps.

This tidbit of advice comes from trying this on a busy day. Advance Preparation is a key.

1. 1 1/2 cups of mild onions like Walla Walla Sweets.
2. 3 medium tomatoes thinly sliced. (Optional)
3. 2 green peppers thinly sliced. Other vegetables like broccoli can be used for your preference or as available.
4. 2 bunches of watercress. If not available, use parsley.
5. 3 leeks quartered, 1/2 pound mushrooms, 1 cup green peas.
6. One pound lean, organic beef or chicken breasts thinly sliced.
7. 1/2 cup sesame oil & 1/4 cup rice wine vinegar. If sesame oil is not available, use 1/2 cup olive oil plus 1/2 cup soy sauce. Some recipes suggest using one cup of each of these ingredients.
8. 1/3 cup sherry, 1/2 tsp. finely grated ginger. To cook: Braise meat first until almost pink. Add vegetables and lightly fry. Serve rice and stir fry in separate bowls.

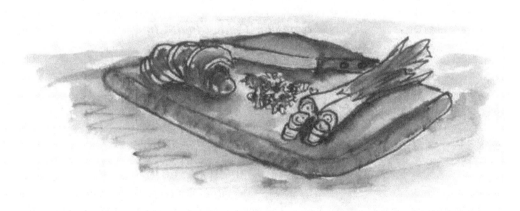

What To Do With Leftovers? Biscuits for Doggie & Kitty?

Your favorite Doggie or Kitty friend will love this one. I use these treats to control my strong willed Rhodesian Ridgeback. Happy will "jump through hoops" for these treats. Yet, everything that goes into the mixture is organic and good for her. Freeze excess to keep it from spoiling immediately and thaw a daily dose to keep fresh.

Chicken Treats & Variations with Beef or Fish scraps. You are now using the same organic foods for him/her that you use for yourself.

After you have made organic chicken soup for your household, clean up the leftover carcass, gristle, skin and any other part of the chicken leftovers that are not bones, etc. From the soup, strain the broth in a colander. Feel through this mash with your fingers to be certain that there are no splinters.

Keep the garlic, celery, onions, parsley, herbs, etc.for the mash that and place this into your food processer. It should make about two cups of mash.

Twirl one and 1/2 cup of oats into a blender to make fine oat flour.

Add this to the mash with two eggs plus 1/4 cup olive oil.

Stir this together. Check the consistency of the mixture. It should be the consistency of a mixed cake mix. Add enough plain oats to create this consistency. I have to play with the mixture at this point, since some chicken leftovers are more soupy and need the extra oats to reach the cake mix level.

Spray an 8 x 10 cake pan with cooking spray. Pour mix into pan. Bake at 350 degrees for 30 minutes or until fork comes clean. Pull from oven. Slice into 1 inch bits. Save one jar for refrigerator. Freeze batches in other jars for later use. Depending upon how often you "reward" your pet, this will last about a month.

Bon Appetit, Fido et Petit Chat!

In A Caravan to See the Sand Hill Cranes.

Undulating, the sand hill cranes follow their leader, gliding the sky. Others join them for their grand reunion over marshes and flats.

We mortals below watch this mysterious oneness of flight as we hike across rocky paths. We wish that we could soar as they do and "churrrr, churrrr, churrr" each other.

We hurry to the flats where we see them preparing to land, hoping to gain a deeper grasp of life in this afternoon vigil as they gather at edge of a world while murrelets and northern shovellers swim.

If we had wings, we'd shed our earthbound expectations for a while and with legs and wings outstretched, we'd fly in "v formations", our haunting calls gathering others to our celebration.

Yes! We would trumpet as they do. We'd jump and bow and spread our dreams across the sky. We'd toss our sticks in crane ballet for joy of friendship. Then we'd start our own symphony as if we had a trachea wrapped like a French horn like they do.

We would play a song like the sand hill cranes in a flute-like sound or check out the coots and egrets who dot the Delta with their "crrr, crrr, crrr."

We spot Trumpeter Swans that beckon to SandHill Cranes with chuckling sounds. It sends our caravan of cars up the road to another site. We listen harder for their message.

Each year these wild ones find the marshes for safe places where predators cannot go.
In hush, they gather to watch other bird migrants arrive on the jetty, while we from city track their pilgrimage across extended fields of rice and grain.

In all glory, one long necked crane sifts stalks of grain for life, even as we sort grains for truth to sustain us for our own u's and v's from God who sends us down our path now -- renewed for another season--

Dec. 2009. With family members.

Container Gardens in Unlikely Places.

Using imagination, you can find places to create a garden, even when you don't have access to a garden plot outside. The following ideas are a way to begin. You'll find other possibilities once you step out of the traditional box of gardening plans. Monitor for under or overwatering. Note: Earth-4 Energy and Hojo Motor = save energy.

Check living spaces for areas that have outdoor light—a window sill or doorway. If not available, consider a grow light or lamp that you can keep lit all day when winter months are cloudy. Even outside of an apartment or on a balcony, a grow box can sometimes fit your needs nicely. This works.

Today, many resources offer ways to purify water and devices that save on electric bills .i.e., This is a fast changing field, so that which might have been suggested even last month is already out of date. If interested, it might be worth the effort to talk to people, check the library and check on the internet.

In the meantime, for growing areas, consider a collection of pots found at garage sales. If you spray paint your orphans to match your décor, you might become your own interior designer. Also, you just might save on grocery dollars.

One example of those creative grow boxes from unusual sources is an antique, low 4' by 8' baby crib found at a garage sale. Large ceramic pots with plants placed inside fit in it and it now rests next to a window. The plants grow well, even though this is not a room with a high outdoor light source. Parsley, chives and lettuce and climbers do well with such an arrangement.

One place on my kitchen countertop also works for starting lettuce plants in the winter. It gives them a head start for later spring growth when the weather outside is warmer.

Keeping Critters at Bay & Other Tidbits.

1. In our garage we were invaded by rats, moths and mice. We got rid of them with bags of bay leaves, lavender and mint leaves throughout the attic and garage. We also left lavender and rat traps in our courtyard, which kept them out of those areas. If you have a dog or cat who snacks on anything, be careful about rat poison. The bay, mint and lavender would probably not harm them.

2. These tidbits worked for the smaller critters, but the raccoons still climbed on the roof and tore away shingles. By spraying them with a product called, "Critter Ridder", we persuaded the raccoons to leave. This is a natural, if unpleasant, spray that can be used for raccoons and other wild animals. An electronic device might also help. It emits sounds animals don't like. Also, get to know local grange suppliers for ideas.

3. Jerry Baker's tips in <u>Green Grass Magic</u> and other books listed at <Jerry Baker.com>. <u>Reader's Digest</u> <u><1001 Do-It-Yourself Hints & Tips></u>, <u>Prevention Magazine's</u> ideas can also help.

4. For a headstart on spring planting, use pots in the kitchen for seeds or use a gauzy material called, "Cloud Cover" outside. This helps protect plants against a light frost. It may not be enough for snow or heavy frost.

5. Consider growing some food where you can "Eat Your Landscaping." Herbs, strawberries, lavender, marjoram, rosemary, tarragon, anise, fruit trees, cactus plants, parsley, etc., can fit into a landscape plan. I had the local B & B nursery set up a landscape design with soil recommendations. The results were worth the effort.

Remember that these ideas worked for one person. The main idea for your plan is. One that fits your needs and pocketbook.

Folk Remedies.
Old Time Tips for Bumps and Glitches in life.
Not meant for any condition where a visit to the doctor is indicated.

An Apple a Day keeps doctor away. Dip apple slices into almond butter or chocolate increases nutrition. See chocolate dip recipe.

Sources of B vitamins = whole grains, eggs, fish (particularly salmon).

If you have trouble sleeping, try lettuce juice. Boil and strain 2 cups of organic lettuce leaves with 1/4 cup mint leaves. Drink in the evening or with dinner. *Zzzzzzz*'s come easier for many.

Tummy soother? For some, Mustard and olive oil with dinner seems to help. Add to salad dressing or on fish or meat. (See salad dressing recipes. Some cultures also use aloe vera extract.

For minor burns, try rubbing cucumbers or leeks on edge of burn. If serious, consult physician. This is not intended as a replacement for medical advice. Folk remedies do not replace medical advice.

Minor cuts. Try rubbing raw garlic on small cut. Emu oil is also used by some tribes for this. (Also helps soften wrinkles.)

Aches and pains. 1/2 cup cinnamon sticks boiled with 1/2 cup ginger covered by tap water. Reduce to 1/2 cup of liquid and sip six times a day. If aches and pains diminish, consider continuing, but be sensitive to times when a doctor's visit is needed.

Baking soda and warm water for upset tummy. Doctors want us to pay attention to our bodies and still take care of ourselves on a daily basis. That will hopefully keep us spending less time in Emergency Rooms. *However, we need to stay aware of when we need to get help, rather than letting a condition get out of control.*

Need quick energy? Eat a pickle instead of candy.

1 tbsp. local honey daily may help some people with allergies. *Not a substitute for medical treatment, when needed.*

Resources.

One line of defense for a healthy life style is to find a physician in harmony with how you view prevention as a part of your life plan. Some doctors are listed as Alternative doctors or Holistic doctors in Yellow Pages. Work with your doctor, so that what you do is balanced. Companies making a difference that have completed much research are:

A. Mannatech. Organic nutritional supplements. Websites =<www.navig8. biz/ SusanCoons1>= for the site for women or <www.navig8.biz/Susan Coons4 = for weight loss. Other sites also for sciences of foods and carbohydrate control, etc. Also: 1-800-645-8088. Mention this book for special discounts often available.

B. Dr. Whitaker., MD. Whitaker Clinic. 1-888-886-8213. They ship. <drwhitaker. com>

C. Dr. David Williams. Mountain Home Nutritionals. Daily Advantage Vitamins. Also, Editor of Alternatives._ 1-800-888-1415 or 800-527-3044. <Dr, davidwilliams.com>

D. <Easy Water.com> Website gives information about clean water. This company started business 25 years ago.1-877-438-5149.

E. Lombardi. Doctor's Health Press. #177, More medical information. 60 State St., Ste. 700, Boston, MA 02109-1894.

F. Energy = Hojo Motor on internet. Also check local Farm Bureau.

G. The Miracles of Apple Cider Vinegar. Drs. Paul & Patricia Bragg.

H. Dr. Jonathan Wright, MD. Library of Food and Vitamin Cures. 1-630-236-4630. www.wrightnewsletter.com. Nutrition Newsletter. Linus Pauline Award. Learn of sugar differences.

I. The Doctor's Book of Food Remedies. Rodale Press. Selena Yeager. 1-800-848-4735. .

J. Jerry Baker's Green Grass Magic. <www.jerrybaker.com> or P.O. Box 805. New Hudson, MI 48165.

K. Mayo Clinic. <Mayo Clinic.com> or:1-507-284-2511 or 200 First St. Rochester, MN 55905 **L.** Reader's Digest. 1001 Do-It-Yourself Hints. Pleasantville, NY. 1-800-304-2807.

M Health Science Institute. Members only Call: 1- 630-236-4529, for membership.

N. Agora Health. *Better Living*. 819 Charles St., Baltimore, MD 21201.Ask for Booklet Doctor's Most Powerful Kitchen Cures.

O. Catherine's Choice. Aloe Vera Supplements since 1981.

P. Seeds grown in USA. Most = non GMO.

1. "Totally Tomatoes" for large assortment of tomatoes. Call 1-800-546-1679.

2. **Garden's Alive** at <www.Garden's Alive>

3. Email or call **Gurney's Seed** company for a full selection of seeds at <www. Gurney's.com> or 1-800-354-1492. For other companies, keep sleuthing and ask questions about where and how seeds are raised. GMO? Non GMO? Avoid China or Russia due to questions of sprays, etc.

Q. Dr. Susan Lark. <u>149 Astonishing Healing Secrets Just For Women</u>. <drlark. com> Supplement to her newsletter.

R. Weight Loss Programs. 10 Minute Trainer.TV infomercial for 4 month program. Weight loss, exercise & diet tips. Optional online support. Call 1-800-108-7964. Many other good programs like Weight Watchers and local gyms. Mannatech also carries an OsoLean program where many report successes.

S. Kyani. Name of a company that also offers a healthy food supplement series. If you are interested in this nutritional product go to: <http: // s_coons@ kyani.net> for a discount. You can also check out the website <www.kyaniscience. net> for general information on the research and history of how this food supplement was developped, based on what the Tlingit tribe in Alaska uses to maintain their healthy longevity.

A key to remember is: "To make a change, we may need to do what we have never done--or we'll get what we've always gotten in the past."

Another Tip: One bottom line for any supplements that we try might be the question, "Does this work for me given an orderly use over a reasonable period of time?" --Dan Swindell.

Tips. Kitchen Gardens & Other Spots

1. **Use containers like an old cradle or crib or a favorite large vase**. Can be on kitchen counter also. Grown in pots, these plants can do well as long if fertilized, but not overwatered, and when they get light from a window or a bulb kept lit during the day. Use quality potting soil. Good reason for a compost pile, if space for it. Friendly guests: Parsley, Chives, Cressa, Butter Lettuce, Kale, Bib Lettuce, Swiss Chard, Basil, Boston Lettuce, lettuce like Radiccio & Arugula.

2. **Plants that prefer the outdoors.** Some of the plants below will survive mild cold when mulched or protected with "Cloud Cover" or other light cloth. Carrot, Cabbage, Beets, Beans, Broccoli, Cauliflower, Brussel Sprouts, Egg Plant, Peas. New Zealand Spinach (rugged plant), Tomatoes, Potatoes, Asparagus. Melons need a hot climate unless you keep them warm with devices like solar panels.

3. **Unlikely spots**. Using imagination, find places for a garden even when you don't have access to an outside plot. For example: In house, check areas that receive outdoor light such as a window or glass doorway. A grow light works well in some areas if lit all day.

4. **Outside shelters.** Even outside of an apartment on a balcony, a grow box can often fit. Experiment to see what does well in your area.

5. **Consider collecting interesting pots from garage sales.** In one area I had a collection of odd pots that looked like they were related when spray painted a nice gray to match the outside of the house. **On the kitchen counter** parsley and lettuce can add to your winter salad bowl. You can save a bit on the budget by supplementing what you get at the store. The bonus here is that you know how "organic" your greens are. If your only use for your kitchen counter is to start seeds for the spring garden, getting a head start on summer can help.

6. **Garden Clubs**. In most villages and cities, you can track down where the garden clubs meet for the bonus of sharing garden tips that fit your region. Gardeners often enjoy sharing their excess seedlings at a very small or no cost, so that everyone gains a bonus from the camaraderie. The best part of the experience is to gain from the wisdom of those designated as "Master Gardeners." (That might be you one day, once you catch the "gardening bug.")

7. **Farmer's Markets**. In many areas, local farmers like to bring vegetables, fruits, eggs to sell once or twice a week. Getting fresh local produce adds the chance to talk with the farmers and gain even more tips. Our local Farmer's Market even features fresh breads and rolls often baked early that morning.

8. **Sense of Community**. At a time when people are looking for ways to gain a sense of connectection, these garden groups and farmer's markets offer another way to meet people. You might even form friendships that are based on mutual interests in fun, wholesome adventures.

9. **Stretching That Dollar $$$$$$$$$$$$$$$$$....**In these economic times the obvious money savings that can come when we find ways to grow our own cannot be overemphasized.

10. **Quality Control**. The bonus of being able to minimize the sprays on your vegetables can help in promoting health for you and those in your household. Research released on the effect of chemicals on foods as a trigger for some cancers makes what you do to keep chemical use at a minimum even more important. Give yourself a brownie point, if you are already doing this.

Cookie Magic? Family members might not be excited when you start or increase your project of health awareness. I made some cookies using the oatmeal flour strategies in recipes and shared them with my neighbor. She then shared them with her grandchildren. They did not like those "healthy" cookies. They were used to local fast food delicacies and wanted no changes. On the other hand, the telephone repairman with whom I shared the cookies said that those same cookies were fabulous. He shared them with a buddy who also loved the cookies and used them for breakfast. The point here is that we can learn not to get upset, when this adventure does not excite everyone. If the neighbor's grandchildren had been my own, I would have baked a cookie that resembled what they normally eat, but would have eliminated the worst poor health trigger--that of sugar. By using a gluten free flour for the base with the addition of slipping in some of the ground oatmeal flour as a filler and adding honey or agave for sweeteners plus raisins, nuts and other seeds we can still get good nutrients back into the mixture.

Butter, according to major clinics, butter is still ok for cooking and health wise for many people, it is better than some of the substitutes for health. The Mayo Clinic recently published its own report that stated that butter might be getting a bad rap. You might check this out as the research reports continue to develop for this arena.